The Splendor of Tradition: Exploring Men's Traditional Attire in India

Welcome to "The Splendor of Tradition: Exploring Men's Traditional Attire in India." In this book, we embark on a fascinating journey through the rich and diverse world of traditional Indian attire for men. India is a land of vibrant cultural heritage, and its clothing traditions reflect the country's history, customs, and regional diversity.

From the regal elegance of the sherwani to the colorful charm of the kurta-pajama, Indian men's traditional clothing is a testament to the artistry, craftsmanship, and intricate detailing that has been passed down through generations. These garments not only showcase the sartorial excellence of Indian fashion but also encapsulate the stories, rituals, and beliefs deeply woven into the fabric of Indian society.

Through this book, we delve into the history, symbolism, and significance of various traditional outfits worn by Indian men. We explore the diverse styles, fabrics, embellishments, and accessories that make each ensemble unique to its region or occasion. From the royal attires of Rajasthan and Gujarat to the understated elegance of South Indian dhoti and angavastram, we uncover the distinct characteristics and cultural contexts of each attire.

"The Splendor of Tradition" is not just a visual feast but also a celebration of the values, customs, and identities associated with Indian men's traditional clothing. It offers insights into the rituals, ceremonies, festivals, and everyday life where these attires play a significant role.

Whether you are an admirer of Indian culture, a fashion enthusiast, or simply curious about the rich heritage of Indian attire, this book invites you to embark on a captivating exploration. Join us as we unravel the captivating tales behind each garment, shedding light on the enduring splendor of tradition in Indian men's attire.

I. Introduction

- Importance of traditional attire in Indian culture
- Significance of preserving and promoting traditional Indian attire for men

II. Historical Background

- Evolution of traditional men's attire in different regions of India
- Influence of historical events and cultural exchange on traditional attire

III. Regional Variations

- Overview of traditional attire in North India
- Traditional attire in South India
- Traditional attire in East India
- Traditional attire in West India
- Unique attire styles in Central India and Northeast India

IV. Key Components of Traditional Attire

- Upper garments
  - Kurta and sherwani
  - Bandhgala
  - Achkan and angrakha
- Lower garments
  - Dhoti and lungi
  - Pajama and churidar
  - Mundu and veshti
- Headgear and turbans
- Footwear and accessories

V. Symbolism and Cultural Significance

- Colors and patterns
- Embroidery and embellishments
- Religious and ceremonial attire
- Social status and community identification

VI. Contemporary Adaptations and Fusion

- Influence of Western fashion on traditional attire
- Fusion of traditional and modern elements in men's clothing
- Role of Bollywood and fashion designers in promoting traditional attire

VII. Revival and Preservation Efforts

- Organizations and initiatives promoting traditional Indian attire
- Government support and cultural festivals
- Fashion shows and exhibitions showcasing traditional attire

VIII. Styling Tips and Guidelines

- Dressing for different occasions and events

- Matching accessories and footwear
- Tips for maintaining and caring for traditional attire

IX. Conclusion

- Reflection on the significance of traditional Indian attire for men
- Call to embrace and preserve the rich heritage of Indian clothing

Importance of traditional attire in Indian culture

Traditional attire holds immense importance in Indian culture as it is not merely a form of clothing but a reflection of history, identity, and values. It serves as a symbol of cultural pride, connecting individuals to their roots and heritage. Here are some key reasons why traditional attire is significant in Indian culture:

1. Preservation of Heritage: Traditional attire plays a crucial role in preserving and showcasing the diverse cultural heritage of India. Each region has its unique clothing styles, fabrics, colors, and embellishments, representing the distinct traditions and customs of that particular area.

2. Cultural Identity: Wearing traditional attire allows individuals to express their cultural identity and affiliation. It serves as a visual marker, indicating one's belonging to a specific community, caste, or region. It fosters a sense of pride and belonging among individuals, fostering a strong connection to their cultural roots.

3. Rituals and Festivals: Traditional attire is an integral part of religious rituals, festivals, and ceremonies in India. From the elaborate wedding rituals to religious celebrations and festive occasions, specific garments are worn to signify the auspiciousness and sacredness of the event. These attires add color, vibrancy, and a sense of occasion to the festivities.

4. Symbolism and Significance: Traditional attire often

carries deep symbolic meaning. The choice of fabric, colors, motifs, and patterns may represent social status, marital status, occupation, or specific beliefs and customs. It serves as a visual language, conveying messages and stories embedded in the attire.

5. Handicraft and Artistry: Indian traditional attire is renowned for its intricate craftsmanship, weaving techniques, and embellishments. Many traditional garments involve labor-intensive processes, such as hand weaving, block printing, embroidery, and textile dyeing. By embracing traditional attire, individuals contribute to the preservation of these ancient craft traditions and support the artisans and craftsmen.

6. Sense of Unity: Traditional attire creates a sense of unity and solidarity among people. During cultural events, festivals, or national celebrations, seeing a multitude of individuals dressed in their traditional attire fosters a sense of community and shared identity. It serves as a visual reminder of the rich cultural diversity that exists within the country.

In summary, traditional attire holds significant cultural, social, and historical value in Indian society. It embodies the essence of India's cultural heritage, acts as a symbol of identity and pride, and serves as a visual language that communicates stories, traditions, and values. It is an integral part of Indian culture, bringing together people from diverse backgrounds and celebrating the timeless splendor of tradition.

Significance of preserving and promoting traditional Indian attire for men

Preserving and promoting traditional Indian attire for men is crucial for several reasons. Here are some key points highlighting the significance of this endeavor:

1. Cultural Heritage: Traditional Indian attire for men is a vital part of India's rich cultural heritage. Each region in India has its own distinct styles, fabrics, and techniques that have been passed down through generations. By preserving and promoting traditional attire, we ensure the continuation of this cultural legacy and keep alive the traditions and customs associated with it.

2. Identity and Pride: Traditional attire plays a pivotal role in shaping individual and collective identities. It serves as a visual representation of one's cultural background, community, and heritage. By wearing traditional Indian attire, men can express their pride in their roots and contribute to the preservation of their cultural identity.

3. Connection to the Past: Traditional Indian attire holds a connection to the past, reflecting the history, customs, and way of life of earlier generations. By embracing and wearing traditional attire, men can reconnect with their cultural roots and carry forward the legacy of their ancestors.

4. Artistry and Craftsmanship: Traditional Indian attire showcases the exceptional craftsmanship and artistic skills of Indian artisans. From handwoven fabrics to intricate embroideries and embellishments, these

garments exemplify the mastery and dedication of skilled craftsmen. Preserving and promoting traditional attire provides economic opportunities for artisans and helps sustain these traditional craft practices.

5. Cultural Exchange and Appreciation: Traditional Indian attire serves as a bridge for cultural exchange and appreciation. By promoting these attires, we create opportunities for people from different cultures to engage, learn, and appreciate the rich diversity of Indian traditions. It fosters a sense of mutual respect and understanding among individuals from different backgrounds.

6. Revitalizing Local Economies: The preservation and promotion of traditional Indian attire contribute to the growth and sustainability of local economies. It provides employment opportunities for artisans, weavers, and other related industries, thereby supporting the local communities and contributing to the overall socio-economic development.

7. Fashion and Style: Traditional Indian attire has a timeless charm and elegance. By incorporating elements of traditional attire into contemporary fashion, men can create unique and stylish ensembles that blend tradition and modernity. This not only showcases their fashion sensibility but also helps in keeping traditional attire relevant and appealing to younger generations.

In conclusion, preserving and promoting traditional Indian attire for men is crucial for safeguarding cultural heritage, fostering identity and pride, supporting artisans and local economies, and promoting cultural exchange. It is through these efforts that we can ensure the longevity and vitality of traditional Indian attire, allowing it to evolve and thrive while retaining its essence and significance.

Evolution of traditional men's attire in different regions of India

The evolution of traditional men's attire in different regions of India is a fascinating journey that showcases the diversity and richness of Indian culture. Here is an overview of the distinctive styles and variations of traditional men's attire across various regions:

1. North India:
   - Punjab: The traditional attire for men includes the kurta, pajama, and a colorful turban called the pagri or dastar.
   - Rajasthan: Men often wear the dhoti or churidar with a long shirt known as the angarkha or kurta.
   - Uttar Pradesh: The traditional attire includes the kurta-pajama or dhoti-kurta, often paired with a Nehru jacket or a sherwani for special occasions.
2. South India:
   - Kerala: Men commonly wear the mundu, a white or cream-colored dhoti, along with a shirt called the jubba or kurta.
   - Tamil Nadu: The traditional attire comprises the veshti or dhoti and a shirt called the angavastram or melmundu.
   - Karnataka: Men often wear the dhoti or panche with a shirt known as the panche kachche.
3. East India:

- West Bengal: The traditional attire for men includes the dhoti, kurta, and a shawl called the gamcha. On special occasions, men wear the dhoti with a silk kurta known as the panjabi.
- Odisha: Men traditionally wear the dhoti with a shirt called the kurta or dhothi kurta. The outfit is often paired with an intricately designed shawl called the uttariya.

4. West India:

- Gujarat: The traditional attire for men includes the dhoti or dhoti-kurta ensemble. Men also wear the kediyu, a short jacket-like garment, over the dhoti.
- Maharashtra: Men often wear the dhoti or pajama with a kurta and a traditional waistcoat called the Bandi or Nehru jacket.
- Rajasthan: In addition to the Rajput-style attire mentioned earlier, Rajasthan is also known for the vibrant turbans worn by men, representing their community and social status.

5. Northeast India:

- Assam: Men traditionally wear the dhoti, a shirt called the kurta or gamosa, and a shawl known as the gamosa.
- Manipur: The traditional attire for men includes the dhoti with a waistcoat called the achkan or a long coat known as the phanek.

It's important to note that these descriptions provide a general overview, and there may be further variations within each region based on subcultures, communities, and occasions. The evolution of traditional men's attire in India reflects the cultural, historical, and regional influences that have shaped the diverse clothing traditions we see today.

Influence of historical events and cultural exchange on traditional attire

The evolution of traditional men's attire in India has been influenced by historical events and cultural exchanges over centuries. Here are some key influences that have shaped traditional Indian attire:

1. Colonial Era: The colonial period in India, particularly under British rule, had a significant impact on Indian attire. Western clothing styles and norms were introduced and adopted by some sections of society, especially in urban areas. This led to the fusion of traditional Indian elements with Western styles, giving rise to new forms of attire.

2. Mughal Influence: The Mughal Empire, which ruled parts of India from the 16th to the 19th century, greatly influenced Indian attire. The Mughal rulers and their courtiers introduced Persian and Central Asian styles, such as the use of luxurious fabrics, intricate embroidery, and draped garments like the angarkha and jama. These influences can still be seen in traditional attire worn during weddings and festive occasions.

3. Cultural Exchange with neighboring countries: India shares cultural and historical connections with neighboring countries like Pakistan, Bangladesh, Sri Lanka, and Nepal. Cultural exchange between these regions has influenced traditional attire. For example, the sherwani worn by Indian grooms finds its roots in Central Asian and Persian styles, while the lungi worn in

South India has similarities with garments worn in Sri Lanka and Bangladesh.

4. Regional Diversity: India's vast geographical expanse and diverse regional cultures have contributed to the varied traditional attire across the country. Each region has its unique clothing styles, influenced by local customs, climate, and historical events. The traditional attire reflects the traditions, beliefs, and occupations of the communities residing in those regions.

5. Festivals and Rituals: Religious festivals and rituals have played a crucial role in shaping traditional attire. For instance, during Diwali, men may wear traditional outfits like the dhoti-kurta or kurta-pajama, while during Eid, Muslim men often wear traditional garments like the kurta, pajama, and sherwani.

6. Socio-Political Movements: Socio-political movements in Indian history, such as the Swadeshi movement during the freedom struggle, promoted the use of indigenous textiles and clothing to resist British dominance. This led to a revival of traditional attire and the promotion of handloom and khadi fabrics.

Overall, historical events, cultural exchanges, regional diversity, and socio-political movements have all played a significant role in shaping the evolution of traditional men's attire in India. These influences have enriched the cultural fabric of the country and continue to inspire contemporary fashion designers and enthusiasts to preserve and reinterpret traditional Indian clothing in modern contexts.

Overview of traditional attire in North India

North India boasts a rich tapestry of traditional attire that reflects the diverse cultural heritage of the region. Here is an overview of some key traditional attire in North India:

1. Sherwani: The sherwani is a long, coat-like garment that originated in the Mughal era. It is typically worn over a kurta and churidar or dhoti, accompanied by a turban or a traditional headgear known as a pagdi. Sherwanis are often embellished with intricate embroidery and are commonly worn by grooms during weddings and festive occasions.

2. Kurta-Pajama: The kurta-pajama is a popular and versatile attire in North India. It consists of a knee-length tunic-style top called a kurta, paired with loose-fitting pants known as pajama. The kurta can be plain or adorned with embroidery, and it is often made from cotton or silk fabric. This attire is suitable for both formal and casual occasions.

3. Achkan: The achkan is a traditional long coat that is typically worn over a kurta and churidar or dhoti. It features a Mandarin collar and can be intricately embroidered or embellished with buttons and tassels. The achkan is commonly worn by men during weddings and formal events.

4. Nehru Jacket: The Nehru jacket is a sleeveless jacket with a Mandarin collar, named after India's first Prime Minister, Jawaharlal Nehru. It is a versatile garment that

can be worn over a kurta or a shirt, adding a touch of elegance to the attire. Nehru jackets are often made from silk, brocade, or other rich fabrics.

5. Pathani Suit: The Pathani suit is a two-piece outfit comprising a knee-length kurta and loose-fitting pants. It is commonly worn in North India and is influenced by Afghan and Pakistani clothing styles. The Pathani suit is popular as casual attire and is often seen during festive celebrations and cultural events.

6. Phiran: The phiran is a loose, long-sleeved cloak-like garment worn in the Kashmir region. It is typically made from wool to provide warmth in the cold mountainous climate. Phirans are adorned with intricate embroidery and are commonly worn by both men and women during festivals and weddings.

These are just a few examples of the traditional attire in North India. The region's rich cultural diversity gives rise to a wide range of clothing styles, each with its unique features and significance. These traditional attires continue to be cherished and celebrated, preserving the cultural heritage of the region.

Traditional attire in South India

South India is known for its vibrant and diverse culture, and traditional attire plays a significant role in showcasing the rich heritage of the region. Here is an overview of traditional attire in South India:

1. Dhoti: The dhoti is a garment that consists of a long piece of cloth wrapped around the waist and legs. It is commonly worn by men in South India, especially during religious ceremonies and traditional functions. The dhoti is made from various fabrics like cotton, silk, or linen, and the style of draping may vary across different states.

2. Veshti/Lungi: The veshti, also known as lungi, is a versatile garment worn by men in South India. It is a rectangular piece of cloth that is wrapped around the waist and reaches the ankles. The veshti is typically made of cotton and is known for its comfort and ease of movement. It is often worn as everyday attire or during special occasions.

3. Kurta: The kurta is a loose-fitting, knee-length tunic that is paired with a dhoti or pajama. It is commonly worn by men in South India and is often made from cotton or silk fabric. The kurta can be plain or adorned with intricate embroidery, depending on the occasion and personal style.

4. Angavastram: The angavastram is a decorative piece of cloth that is draped over one shoulder and worn as an accessory. It is often made from silk and is commonly seen during religious ceremonies and festivals. The

angavastram adds a touch of elegance to the traditional attire and is considered a symbol of respect and auspiciousness.

5. Mundu: The mundu is a traditional garment worn by men in Kerala. It is similar to the dhoti but is usually white in color. The mundu is draped around the waist and is worn with or without a shirt. It is a staple attire for formal occasions and cultural events in Kerala.

6. Jubba: The jubba is a loose-fitting, knee-length tunic that is often worn by men in South India. It is typically made from cotton or silk and can be plain or adorned with simple embroidery. The jubba is a comfortable and stylish attire for formal gatherings and festivals.

These are some of the traditional attires in South India that showcase the cultural diversity and heritage of the region. The unique styles and fabrics used in these garments reflect the traditions and customs that have been passed down through generations, making them an integral part of South Indian culture.

Traditional attire in East India

East India is known for its rich cultural heritage, and traditional attire in this region reflects the diverse ethnic groups and their unique customs. Here is an overview of traditional attire in East India:

1. Dhoti and Kurta: Dhoti and kurta are commonly worn by men in East India. The dhoti is a long piece of cloth wrapped around the waist and legs, while the kurta is a loose-fitting, knee-length tunic. This combination is popular among men for festivals, weddings, and other traditional occasions. The dhoti and kurta can be made of cotton, silk, or other fabrics, and may feature intricate designs or embroidery.

2. Gamcha: The gamcha is a traditional scarf or towel that is commonly worn around the neck or draped over the shoulders in East India. It is made of cotton and comes in various colors and patterns. The gamcha serves both as a functional accessory for wiping sweat and as a decorative element to enhance the traditional attire.

3. Pajama and Sherwani: Pajama, a loose-fitting trouser, is often paired with a sherwani, which is a long coat-like garment. This combination is worn by men during special occasions such as weddings and formal events. Sherwanis are typically made of silk or brocade and are embellished with intricate embroidery and embellishments.

4. Topor: In East India, especially in West Bengal, the topor is a traditional headgear worn by grooms during weddings. It is typically made of shola (a type of

sponge wood) and adorned with decorative elements like flowers and ornaments. The topor holds cultural significance and is considered a symbol of marital bliss and prosperity.

5. Dhuti and Panjabi: Dhuti, also known as dhoti, is a traditional garment worn by men in West Bengal and other parts of East India. It is a long piece of cloth wrapped around the waist and legs, similar to the dhoti worn in other regions. The panjabi is a knee-length tunic that is worn over the dhuti. This ensemble is often worn during festivals, cultural events, and religious ceremonies.

6. Gamosa: Gamosa is a traditional Assamese cloth that is commonly worn as a scarf or towel by men in Assam. It is usually made of cotton and features intricate designs and patterns. The gamosa holds cultural significance and is used in various rituals and ceremonies in Assam.

These are some of the traditional attires in East India that reflect the cultural diversity and heritage of the region. The unique styles, fabrics, and accessories associated with these attires showcase the distinct identities and traditions of the different communities in East India.

Traditional attire in West India

West India is a region rich in cultural diversity, and traditional attire in this part of the country reflects the unique heritage and customs of various communities. Here is an overview of traditional attire in West India:

1. Kurta and Dhoti: Kurta, a loose-fitting tunic, and dhoti, a long piece of cloth wrapped around the waist and legs, are commonly worn by men in West India. This combination is popular for festive occasions, weddings, and religious ceremonies. The dhoti can be plain or adorned with colorful patterns, while the kurta can be made of cotton, silk, or other fabrics and may feature intricate embroidery or block prints.

2. Bandhgala Suit: The Bandhgala suit is a traditional formal attire for men in West India. It is a tailored suit with a high collar and buttons running down the front. The suit is usually paired with trousers and is often made of silk, brocade, or other luxurious fabrics. Bandhgala suits are worn on special occasions, including weddings, receptions, and cultural events.

3. Gujarati Traditional Attire: In Gujarat, the traditional attire for men includes the kediyu and dhoti. The kediyu is a short-sleeved, pleated blouse-like garment, while the dhoti is a long piece of cloth wrapped around the waist and legs. This attire is often embellished with colorful embroidery and mirror work, showcasing the rich craftsmanship of Gujarat.

4. Rajasthani Traditional Attire: In Rajasthan, men often wear a traditional outfit consisting of a long-sleeved

kurta, dhoti or breeches, and a colorful turban known as a pagri or safa. The kurta may be plain or adorned with intricate embroidery and mirror work. The pagri is an essential accessory that represents the wearer's social status and is available in various styles and colors.

5. Pathani Suit: The Pathani suit is a traditional attire commonly worn by men in Maharashtra and other parts of West India. It consists of a loose-fitting, knee-length tunic known as a kurta and matching trousers. The Pathani suit is often made of silk or cotton and is worn on festive occasions and cultural events.

6. Kolhapuri Chappals: Kolhapuri chappals are traditional handcrafted leather sandals that originated in Maharashtra. They are known for their durability and unique designs. Kolhapuri chappals are often worn with traditional attire in West India, adding a touch of authenticity to the overall look.

These are some examples of traditional attire in West India that showcase the region's cultural diversity and heritage. Each style of attire represents the unique traditions and customs of the communities in West India and reflects the artistic craftsmanship and vibrant colors of the region.

Unique attire styles in Central India and Northeast India

Central India and Northeast India have distinct cultures and traditions, which are reflected in their unique traditional attire for men. Here is an overview of traditional attire in these regions:

Central India:

1. Bundi and Banda: Bundi and Banda are traditional attires worn by men in Madhya Pradesh and Chhattisgarh. Bundi is a sleeveless jacket with intricate embroidery or mirror work, worn over a kurta or shirt. Banda is a long scarf-like garment draped over the shoulder and can be made of silk or cotton.

2. Paghdi: Paghdi or turban is a significant accessory in Central India. The turban styles vary from region to region and represent the wearer's community or social status. They are often embellished with ornaments, brooches, or feathers.

3. Dhoti and Angarkha: Dhoti, a piece of cloth wrapped around the waist and legs, is commonly worn in Central India. It is paired with an angarkha, a loose-fitting top with overlapping panels that are fastened with strings or buttons.

Northeast India:

1. Mekhela Chador: Mekhela Chador is a traditional attire worn by men in Assam. It consists of a mekhela, a rectangular piece of cloth worn as a lower garment, and

a chador, which is draped over the shoulders. Mekhela Chador is often made of silk with intricate motifs and designs.

2. Gamosa: Gamosa is a traditional towel-like cloth with intricate designs and patterns, primarily worn in Assam. It is draped around the neck or used as a headgear during cultural and religious ceremonies.

3. Japi: Japi is a traditional hat made of bamboo and covered with colorful fabric or designs. It is commonly worn by men in Assam as a part of their traditional attire.

4. Puan: Puan is a traditional wraparound skirt worn by men in Mizoram and other states of Northeast India. It is made of handwoven fabric with vibrant patterns and designs.

5. Dhoti-Kurta: Dhoti and kurta are also worn by men in some parts of Northeast India, particularly in Manipur and Nagaland. The dhoti is wrapped around the waist and legs, while the kurta is a loose-fitting tunic worn on top.

These are some examples of unique attire styles in Central India and Northeast India. Each style carries cultural significance, reflecting the traditions, customs, and artistic heritage of these regions. The attire not only showcases the diversity of India but also represents the identity and pride of the people in Central and Northeast India.

Kurta and sherwani

Kurta and Sherwani are two popular traditional attires for men in India, commonly worn during special occasions and festive celebrations. Here's an overview of both:

Kurta: The Kurta is a loose, knee-length shirt that can be paired with various bottom wear like pajamas, dhotis, or jeans. It is made from a wide range of fabrics, including cotton, silk, linen, and synthetic materials. Kurta designs can vary, from simple and casual to elaborately embroidered or embellished for more formal occasions. The neckline and sleeve styles also differ, with options like round neck, collar neck, and full sleeves, three-quarter sleeves, or short sleeves. Kurtas are versatile and can be worn for cultural events, religious ceremonies, weddings, or as casual wear depending on the fabric, design, and occasion.

Sherwani: Sherwani is a long, coat-like garment that originated in the Mughal era and is known for its regal and elegant look. It is typically worn over a kurta or a shirt and paired with bottom wear like churidar or pajamas. Sherwanis are often made from rich fabrics such as silk, brocade, or velvet and are adorned with intricate embroidery, zari work, or embellishments. They are characterized by their fitted and structured silhouette, high collars, long sleeves, and long lengths that usually reach below the knee. Sherwanis are commonly worn by grooms during weddings and other formal occasions, representing a sense of traditional elegance and sophistication.

Both Kurta and Sherwani are important elements of traditional Indian men's attire, showcasing the cultural diversity and heritage of the country. They hold a significant place in Indian fashion and are cherished for their timeless appeal, blending modern trends with traditional aesthetics.

Bandhgala

Bandhgala, also known as the Jodhpuri suit, is a traditional Indian attire for men that has gained popularity both domestically and internationally. Here's an overview of the Bandhgala:

Bandhgala: The Bandhgala is a formal suit consisting of a closed-neck jacket with a mandarin collar, typically worn over a kurta or shirt and paired with trousers. It is characterized by its structured and fitted silhouette, giving a sophisticated and regal appearance. The jacket of the Bandhgala is usually made from rich fabrics like silk, brocade, or velvet and is often adorned with intricate embroidery or embellishments. The trousers are typically straight-cut and tailored to complement the jacket.

The Bandhgala is named after the "bandh" or button closures on the front of the jacket. These buttons can be made from various materials, including metal, fabric-covered, or traditional Indian buttons like the ones made from "mango" or "lotus" seeds. The Bandhgala is considered a versatile ensemble as it can be worn for both formal and semi-formal occasions, such as weddings, receptions, cultural events, or even as part of a groom's attire.

The Bandhgala reflects the fusion of Indian and Western styles, blending traditional elements with contemporary tailoring. It has become a popular choice among fashion-conscious men who seek a combination of elegance, sophistication, and cultural heritage in their attire. The Bandhgala has also gained recognition globally, with its unique design and versatility appealing to individuals seeking an alternative to conventional formal wear.

Overall, the Bandhgala is a classic and timeless attire that showcases the rich cultural heritage of India while offering a stylish and modern take on men's formal fashion.

Achkan and angrakha

Achkan and Angrakha are two distinct traditional Indian attire styles for men. Let's explore each of them:

1. Achkan: Achkan is a long, coat-like garment that is typically worn by men. It is characterized by its knee-length or longer hemline, front opening with buttons or hooks, and a fitted or loose silhouette depending on the style and occasion. The Achkan is usually made from luxurious fabrics like silk, brocade, or velvet, and it can be plain or adorned with intricate embroidery, embellishments, or decorative patterns.

Traditionally, the Achkan was worn as a formal or ceremonial garment, especially by noblemen or individuals of high social status. However, over time, it has evolved into a versatile attire that can be worn for various occasions, ranging from weddings and festive celebrations to cultural events or formal gatherings. It is often paired with a churidar (tight-fitting trousers) or a dhoti (traditional Indian draped garment) to complete the ensemble.

2. Angrakha: Angrakha is a traditional Indian tunic-like garment that is characterized by its asymmetric or overlapping front panels and a tie or knot closure on the side. It is typically knee-length or longer and can have either a loose or fitted silhouette. The Angrakha is traditionally made from fabrics like cotton, silk, or linen, and it can be embellished with block prints, embroidery, or other decorative elements.

The Angrakha has a rich historical significance and was widely worn in various regions of India. It has a regal and elegant appeal and is often associated with traditional festivities, cultural events, and weddings. However, modern variations of the Angrakha have emerged, making it a popular choice for both formal and casual occasions.

Both the Achkan and Angrakha represent the diversity and cultural heritage of India. They showcase intricate craftsmanship, exquisite fabrics, and unique design elements that make them stand out in traditional men's attire. These garments have transcended time and continue to be cherished as a symbol of grace, tradition, and elegance.

Dhoti and lungi

Dhoti and lungi are two traditional Indian garments that have been worn by men for centuries. Let's explore each of them:

1. Dhoti: The dhoti is a long, unstitched cloth that is draped around the waist and legs to create a loose, skirt-like garment. It is typically made from cotton or silk fabric and is available in various colors and patterns. The dhoti is worn by men across different regions of India, but its style and draping technique can vary.

The traditional way of wearing a dhoti involves wrapping the cloth around the waist, bringing it between the legs, and tucking it securely at the back. The remaining fabric is then draped over the shoulder or tucked into the waistband. The dhoti is often paired with a kurta (a long shirt) or a traditional upper garment.

Dhotis are commonly worn during religious ceremonies, festive occasions, weddings, and cultural events. They hold significant cultural and religious symbolism and are considered a symbol of tradition, grace, and masculinity.

2. Lungi: The lungi is a similar garment to the dhoti, but it is typically shorter in length and does not require elaborate draping. It is a rectangular piece of fabric that is wrapped around the waist and tucked securely. The lungi is commonly worn in South India, Bangladesh, and Sri Lanka.

Lungis are usually made from lightweight cotton fabric and are available in a wide range of colors and patterns. They provide comfort and ease of movement, making them suitable for everyday wear, especially in hot and humid climates. Lungis are often worn with a matching or contrasting short-sleeved shirt.

While lungis are primarily worn as casual attire, they can also be seen in rural or traditional settings, informal gatherings, and as sleepwear. They are known for their simplicity, affordability, and practicality.

Both the dhoti and lungi hold cultural significance in Indian society. They represent traditional values, regional diversity, and a connection to India's rich heritage. Despite the modernization of clothing styles, these garments continue to be cherished and worn by men who embrace their cultural roots and appreciate the comfort and elegance they offer.

Pajama and churidar

Pajama and churidar are two traditional bottom wear options for men in India. Let's explore each of them:

1. Pajama: Pajama is a loose-fitting trouser that is typically made from cotton fabric. It is characterized by its comfortable and relaxed fit. Pajamas are usually worn with a kurta, which is a long tunic-like shirt. Together, the pajama and kurta form a popular traditional outfit known as the "kurta pajama."

Pajamas are available in various colors and patterns, and they are often embellished with embroidery or decorative details. They are considered versatile and suitable for both formal and casual occasions. Pajama sets are commonly worn at weddings, festivals, family gatherings, and other cultural events.

2. Churidar: Churidar is a form-fitting lower garment that is typically made from stretchable fabric. It is characterized by its tight fit from the waist to the knees, and then it flares out into folds or gathers at the ankles. Churidars are commonly worn with a kurta or a sherwani.

Churidars are known for their elegance and sophistication. They enhance the overall appearance of the traditional attire and create a sleek and tailored look. Churidars are often made from silk or other luxurious fabrics and are available in a variety of colors and designs.

Churidars are popular choices for special occasions such as weddings, religious ceremonies, and formal gatherings. They are favored for their versatility, as they can be paired with different styles of kurtas or sherwanis to create various traditional looks.

Both pajama and churidar are widely embraced as traditional bottom wear options for men in India. They offer comfort, style, and a sense of cultural identity. Whether it's the relaxed fit of pajamas or the tailored look of churidars, these garments continue to be an integral part of traditional Indian attire, showcasing the rich sartorial heritage of the country.

Mundu and veshti

Mundu and veshti are traditional garments worn by men in the southern regions of India, particularly in Kerala and Tamil Nadu. Let's explore each of them:

1. Mundu: Mundu is a white or off-white garment that is similar to a dhoti. It is a rectangular piece of cotton fabric that is wrapped around the waist and worn as a lower garment. Mundu is typically worn without pleats and is draped in a way that the loose ends are brought forward and tucked in at the waist. It is usually worn with a shirt or a traditional garment known as the "jubba" or "melmundu" in Kerala.

Mundu is considered a symbol of simplicity and purity. It is a comfortable and breathable garment, suitable for the hot and humid climate of southern India. Mundu is commonly worn for religious ceremonies, formal occasions, and cultural events.

2. Veshti: Veshti, also known as dhoti, is a traditional garment that is similar to mundu but typically worn with pleats. It is a long piece of fabric that is wrapped around the waist and then folded to create pleats in the front. The pleats are tucked in at the waist, while the remaining fabric is draped over and around the legs.

Veshti is available in various colors and designs, but white is the most common and traditional choice. It is often paired with a shirt or an upper garment known as the "angavastram." Veshti is considered a symbol of elegance, grace, and tradition. It is commonly worn for religious ceremonies, weddings, festive occasions, and cultural events.

Both mundu and veshti are significant elements of the traditional attire in southern India. They reflect the cultural heritage and customs of the region. The simplicity and versatility of these garments make them popular choices for men, allowing them to embrace their cultural identity and showcase the timeless beauty of traditional Indian attire.

Headgear and turbans

Headgear and turbans play a significant role in traditional Indian attire for men. Let's explore these elements:

1. Pagri/Turban: The turban, also known as pagri or safa, is a headgear that is widely worn in various regions of India. Turbans come in different styles, colors, and materials, reflecting regional and cultural diversity. They are typically worn as a symbol of respect, honor, and tradition.

Turbans are made by wrapping a long piece of cloth around the head in a specific manner. The size, shape, and style of the turban can vary depending on the region and occasion. Different regions in India have their unique turban styles, such as the Rajasthani pagri, Punjabi pagri, or the Mysore peta in Karnataka.

Turbans are commonly worn during weddings, religious ceremonies, and festive occasions. They serve as a symbol of pride, dignity, and cultural identity, representing the rich heritage and traditions of India.

2. Topi/Skull Cap: The topi or skull cap is a smaller headgear worn by Muslim men in India. It is typically a close-fitting cap that covers the top of the head. Topis come in various colors and styles, and they are often made of soft fabrics like cotton or silk.

Topis are an integral part of religious and cultural attire for Muslim men, particularly during prayers, festivals, and other significant occasions. They are a symbol of religious identity and are worn to display faith and modesty.

3. Pheta/Safa: The pheta or safa is a traditional Marathi headgear worn by men in the state of Maharashtra. It is typically a turban-like wrap made of cotton or silk fabric. The pheta is often intricately folded and draped, creating a unique and elegant style.

Phetas are worn on special occasions like weddings, festivals, and cultural events in Maharashtra. They signify honor, tradition, and pride in the Marathi culture.

Headgear and turbans in India are not only fashion statements but also carry cultural, religious, and regional significance. They add a touch of elegance, pride, and identity to traditional men's attire, showcasing the diversity and rich heritage of the country.

Footwear and accessories

In addition to clothing, traditional Indian attire for men also includes unique footwear and accessories. Let's explore some of them:

1. Jutis/Mojris: Jutis or mojris are traditional Indian footwear that have been worn for centuries. They are handcrafted shoes made of leather or fabric and feature intricate embroidery, embellishments, or colorful designs. Jutis are typically flat or have a low heel and are known for their comfort and elegance. They are commonly worn with traditional outfits like kurta-pajama or sherwani and are popular across different regions of India.

2. Kolhapuri Chappals: Kolhapuri chappals originated in the state of Maharashtra and are known for their distinctive style. These sandals are handmade using leather, and their design features intricate braids and patterns. Kolhapuri chappals are durable, comfortable, and have gained popularity not only in India but also internationally.

3. Patka and Safa: Patka and safa are accessories worn on the head, specifically during festive and special occasions. Patka is a small scarf tied around the forehead, while safa is a long cloth tied as a turban. Both of these accessories come in various colors and materials, complementing the traditional attire and adding a touch of elegance to the overall look.

4. Shawls and Stoles: Shawls and stoles are common accessories worn by men in colder regions or during

formal events. They are typically made of fine wool, silk, or cashmere, and come in a wide range of designs, patterns, and colors. Shawls and stoles not only provide warmth but also enhance the visual appeal of traditional attire.

5. Jewelry and Accessories: Men's traditional attire in India also incorporates jewelry and accessories to enhance the overall look. This can include items such as brooches, cufflinks, necklaces, rings, and bracelets. These pieces of jewelry are often made of precious metals like gold or silver and may feature gemstones or intricate designs.

The choice of footwear and accessories may vary depending on the specific region, occasion, and personal style preferences. They add the finishing touches to traditional Indian attire for men, completing the cultural and aesthetic appeal.

Colors and patterns

Colors and patterns play a significant role in traditional Indian attire for men. They not only reflect the cultural heritage but also add vibrancy and symbolism to the garments. Here are some notable aspects related to colors and patterns in traditional Indian attire:

1. Vibrant Colors: Traditional Indian attire for men often features a wide array of vibrant colors. Each color holds its own significance and symbolism. For example, red is associated with celebrations and auspicious occasions, while white is often worn during religious ceremonies or mourning. Other popular colors include blue, green, yellow, and orange, each representing different aspects of Indian culture and traditions.

2. Intricate Patterns and Embroidery: Traditional Indian attire is known for its intricate patterns and exquisite embroidery work. These patterns can vary based on the region, with each having its own unique style. For instance, you may find elaborate floral motifs, paisley designs (known as "mango" patterns), geometric shapes, or traditional motifs inspired by nature, animals, or historical elements. These patterns are often meticulously crafted using techniques like zari (metallic threadwork), zardozi (embroidery with gold and silver threads), or resham (silk thread embroidery).

3. Regional Influence: Different regions of India have their own distinct color palettes and patterns in traditional attire. For example, in North India, vibrant colors like red, maroon, and gold are prominent, while South

Indian attire often features rich gold, white, and earthy tones. East Indian attire incorporates a mix of vibrant colors with intricate handloom designs, while West Indian attire embraces bright colors with mirror work and bandhani tie-dye patterns.

4. Symbolic Meanings: Colors and patterns in traditional Indian attire can also hold symbolic meanings. For instance, in some regions, specific colors may be associated with marital status or social hierarchy. Patterns may represent cultural beliefs, customs, or historical narratives. These symbolic elements add depth and cultural significance to the garments, making them more than just clothing.

The use of colors and patterns in traditional Indian attire for men reflects the rich cultural diversity and artistic heritage of the country. They not only enhance the visual appeal but also convey stories, traditions, and a sense of identity.

Embroidery and embellishments

Embroidery and embellishments are integral aspects of traditional Indian attire for men. They add intricate detailing and exquisite craftsmanship to the garments, enhancing their visual appeal and cultural significance. Here are some key points about embroidery and embellishments in Indian attire:

1. Zari Work: Zari is a type of embroidery that involves the use of metallic threads, usually gold or silver, to create intricate patterns and designs. It is commonly seen in traditional men's attire like sherwanis, kurta-pajamas, and turbans. Zari work adds a touch of opulence and grandeur to the garments, making them suitable for special occasions and celebrations.

2. Zardozi: Zardozi is a type of heavy and elaborate embroidery that originated in Persia and later became popular in India. It involves the use of gold or silver threads, along with beads, sequins, and precious stones, to create intricate patterns and designs. Zardozi work is often found on wedding attire, such as sherwanis and bandhgalas, and imparts a rich and luxurious look to the garments.

3. Resham Embroidery: Resham embroidery, also known as silk thread embroidery, is a popular technique used in traditional Indian attire. It involves the use of silk threads of different colors to create intricate and colorful patterns. Resham embroidery is seen on various garments, including kurta-pajamas, achkans, and jackets. It adds a vibrant and lively touch to the attire.

4. Sequins and Beads: Sequins and beads are commonly used embellishments in Indian attire. They are often hand-sewn onto the fabric to create dazzling patterns and designs. These embellishments add a touch of sparkle and glamour to the garments, making them suitable for festive occasions and special events.

5. Mirror Work: Mirror work, also known as shisha embroidery, is a traditional technique where small mirrors are attached to the fabric using colorful threads. It is commonly found in traditional attire from Gujarat and Rajasthan. Mirror work adds a reflective and eye-catching element to the garments, creating a beautiful play of light.

Embroidery and embellishments in traditional Indian attire showcase the skill and artistry of Indian craftsmen. They not only enhance the aesthetic appeal of the garments but also contribute to the cultural identity and heritage of the region. These intricate details make each piece of attire unique and reflect the rich traditions and craftsmanship of India.

Religious and ceremonial attire

Religious and ceremonial attire holds significant importance in traditional Indian culture. It reflects the religious beliefs, customs, and rituals associated with various faiths practiced in the country. Here are some key points about religious and ceremonial attire in India:

1. Hindu Attire: Hinduism, being the dominant religion in India, has a wide variety of traditional attire for men associated with different ceremonies and rituals. The attire may vary based on the region and specific customs, but common elements include dhotis, kurta-pajamas, and sherwanis. In religious ceremonies, men often wear traditional white dhotis and angavastrams (stoles) while performing rituals or visiting temples.

2. Sikh Attire: Sikh men typically wear a traditional attire called the "Punjabi suit," which consists of a loose-fitting shirt (kurta) and matching pants (churidar) along with a turban (dastaar) that signifies their faith and commitment to Sikh principles. The turban holds great religious and cultural significance for Sikh men and represents their identity and spirituality.

3. Muslim Attire: Muslim men in India often wear traditional attire like the kurta and pajama or the sherwani, especially during religious festivals, weddings, and other special occasions. The traditional cap (topi) or the turban (pagri) is also worn to show respect and adherence to Islamic traditions.

4. Christian Attire: Christian men in India typically wear formal Western-style attire for church services and

religious ceremonies, such as suits, trousers, shirts, and ties. However, in certain regions, especially among the Anglo-Indian community, traditional Indian attire with a touch of Western influence, such as the sherwani or achkan, may be worn for weddings and other special events.

5. Jain and Buddhist Attire: Jain and Buddhist men in India often wear simple and modest attire that reflects their beliefs in non-violence, simplicity, and detachment from material possessions. White or off-white clothing, such as dhotis or robes, is commonly worn during religious ceremonies and meditation practices.

Religious and ceremonial attire in India not only serves as a mark of religious identity but also represents the cultural heritage and values associated with different faiths. It reflects the diversity and richness of India's religious traditions and plays a significant role in religious ceremonies, festivals, weddings, and other special occasions.

Social status and community identification

In traditional Indian society, attire has long been associated with social status and community identification. Different regions and communities in India have their unique styles of attire that signify their cultural heritage and social standing. Here are some key points regarding the influence of attire on social status and community identification:

1. Royal Attire: Historically, royal families and nobility in India had distinct attire that set them apart from the common people. Elaborate and luxurious garments, adorned with intricate embroidery, jewels, and precious metals, were reserved for the royals, indicating their elevated social status and power.

2. Caste-Based Attire: The caste system, although now officially abolished, has had a deep impact on Indian society. In the past, certain castes or communities had specific attire associated with their social standing. The color, fabric, and style of the attire could vary based on caste, and these distinctions helped identify a person's caste affiliation.

3. Regional and Community Attire: Each region and community in India has its traditional attire that reflects its distinct culture, history, and social customs. For example, in North India, the Achkan and sherwani are often worn by grooms during weddings, while in South India, men commonly wear dhotis and lungis. These attire choices help in identifying the wearer's regional background and community affiliation.

4. Professional Attire: Certain professions or occupations

in India have their specific attire that distinguishes them from others. For example, priests in temples wear traditional attire associated with their religious roles, and rural farmers may wear distinct attire suited for their agricultural work. These professional attires contribute to community identification and highlight the wearer's occupation or role in society.

5. Community Celebrations: During festivals and community celebrations, people often dress in traditional attire that is specific to their region or community. This collective display of traditional attire fosters a sense of unity and belonging within the community and reinforces cultural identity.

Attire in India has played a crucial role in signifying social status, community identity, and cultural heritage. While modernization and globalization have brought changes to the way people dress, traditional attire continues to be cherished and worn on special occasions, festivals, weddings, and cultural events as a way of preserving and celebrating Indian traditions and identities.

Influence of Western fashion on traditional attire

The influence of Western fashion on traditional attire in India has been significant, particularly in the modern era. Here are some key points regarding the influence of Western fashion on traditional Indian attire:

1. Introduction of Western Clothing: With the advent of colonial rule in India, Western clothing styles were introduced to the country. Western attire such as shirts, trousers, suits, and dresses gained popularity among certain sections of society, particularly the urban elite and educated classes. This led to a gradual shift in fashion preferences and the adoption of Western clothing in everyday life.

2. Fusion of Traditional and Western Styles: Over time, Indian fashion designers began experimenting with incorporating Western elements into traditional Indian attire. This fusion of styles resulted in the creation of innovative designs that combined the aesthetic sensibilities of both traditions. For example, fusion wear like Indo-Western outfits emerged, which feature traditional Indian silhouettes with Western cuts, fabrics, and embellishments.

3. Influence on Silhouettes and Cuts: Western fashion has influenced the silhouettes and cuts of traditional Indian garments. For instance, the introduction of tailored stitching techniques and fitted styles in men's attire like sherwanis and kurtas has made them more

contemporary and appealing to a wider audience. Similarly, women's attire like sarees and salwar kameezes have seen variations in draping styles and cuts inspired by Western fashion trends.

4. Fabric Choices and Textile Innovation: Western fashion introduced new fabrics and textile techniques to India, leading to innovation and diversification in traditional attire. Fabrics like silk, cotton, and wool were blended with synthetic materials to enhance durability and comfort. Traditional handloom textiles were also modernized to cater to changing fashion preferences and market demands.

5. Influence on Formal and Occasional Attire: Western fashion has had a significant impact on formal and occasional attire in India. For special events like weddings, parties, and red carpet appearances, people often opt for fusion wear, designer outfits, or Western-style suits and gowns. This trend is particularly noticeable among the urban youth and those with a cosmopolitan lifestyle.

6. Globalization and Access to Fashion Trends: The advent of globalization and easy access to fashion trends through the internet and social media platforms has further accelerated the influence of Western fashion on traditional attire. People now have greater exposure to international fashion trends and often incorporate elements of Western fashion into their traditional outfits.

While Western fashion has undoubtedly influenced traditional attire in India, it is important to note that traditional styles and garments continue to hold immense cultural and symbolic value. Many Indians take pride in their heritage and actively seek to preserve and promote traditional attire, often finding a balance between traditional and Western influences to create unique and contemporary fashion expressions.

Fusion of traditional and modern elements in men's clothing

The fusion of traditional and modern elements in men's clothing has become a popular trend in recent years. It involves blending traditional silhouettes, fabrics, and motifs with contemporary styles, cuts, and embellishments to create a unique and sophisticated look. Here are some key aspects of the fusion of traditional and modern elements in men's clothing:

1. Silhouettes and Cuts: Traditional silhouettes like kurtas, sherwanis, and bandhgalas are often given a modern twist by incorporating contemporary cuts and tailoring techniques. Slimmer fits, shorter lengths, and altered proportions add a modern touch to the traditional attire, making it more versatile and suitable for various occasions.

2. Fabrics and Textures: Traditional fabrics like silk, cotton, and linen are often combined with modern textiles such as denim, suede, or leather to create interesting contrasts. This combination of fabrics adds depth and visual appeal to the garment, showcasing a harmonious blend of traditional and modern elements.

3. Embellishments and Details: Traditional men's clothing often features intricate embroideries, embellishments, and handcrafted details. In the fusion of traditional and modern elements, these embellishments are reinterpreted in a contemporary way. For example, traditional zardozi work may be applied to a modern jacket, or hand block printing may be incorporated into

a Western-style shirt.

4. Colors and Patterns: Traditional color palettes and patterns are given a modern twist to create a fresh and updated look. Vibrant hues and bold patterns are often combined with more subtle tones and contemporary prints to strike a balance between tradition and modernity.

5. Accessories and Styling: Accessories play a crucial role in merging traditional and modern elements. Traditional accessories like turbans, stoles, and ethnic footwear can be paired with modern ensembles to create a fusion look. Additionally, contemporary accessories such as watches, belts, and pocket squares can complement traditional attire, adding a touch of modern sophistication.

6. Occasion-specific Fusion Wear: Fusion wear for men is particularly popular for special occasions like weddings, festivals, and cultural events. Men often opt for outfits that combine traditional elements with modern designs to create a unique and stylish look that reflects their cultural heritage while embracing contemporary fashion sensibilities.

The fusion of traditional and modern elements in men's clothing allows individuals to showcase their cultural identity while embracing the changing fashion landscape. It offers a fresh and innovative approach to dressing, appealing to those who appreciate the rich heritage of traditional attire while seeking a modern and relevant style.

Role of Bollywood and fashion designers in promoting traditional attire

Bollywood and fashion designers have played a significant role in promoting traditional attire and bringing it into the mainstream fashion scene. Here are some ways in which they have contributed to the popularity and promotion of traditional attire:

1. Red Carpet Appearances: Bollywood celebrities often don traditional attire for red carpet events, award ceremonies, and film promotions. Their high-profile appearances in exquisite traditional outfits create a buzz and inspire people to embrace and appreciate traditional attire.

2. Film Costumes: Bollywood movies often depict rich cultural traditions and showcase elaborate costumes that represent different regions of India. Costume designers meticulously create stunning ensembles that capture the essence of traditional attire, giving them a platform to reach a wider audience.

3. Fashion Shows and Runways: Fashion designers frequently incorporate traditional elements into their collections and showcase them on prestigious runways and fashion shows. These events provide a platform for designers to showcase their creativity and innovation in blending traditional and modern elements, making traditional attire more accessible and appealing to a global audience.

4. Celebrity Endorsements: Bollywood celebrities are often brand ambassadors for fashion designers and clothing

brands. Their association with traditional attire and their endorsement of specific brands or designers help create a strong association between Bollywood glamour and traditional fashion, influencing consumer choices and increasing the popularity of traditional attire.

5. Fashion Magazine Features: Fashion magazines regularly feature Bollywood celebrities in traditional attire, showcasing the beauty and elegance of these outfits. These features not only highlight the craftsmanship and intricate details of traditional attire but also provide styling inspirations for readers.

6. Social Media Influencers: Bollywood celebrities and fashion designers have a significant presence on social media platforms. Their posts and updates showcasing traditional attire and cultural influences have a massive reach and impact, influencing trends and inspiring people to incorporate traditional elements into their wardrobes.

Through their influence and reach, Bollywood and fashion designers have been instrumental in creating awareness, appreciation, and demand for traditional attire. They have successfully blended traditional aesthetics with contemporary fashion, making traditional attire more relevant, accessible, and appealing to a diverse audience.

Organizations and initiatives promoting traditional Indian attire

There are several organizations and initiatives that are actively involved in promoting traditional Indian attire. These organizations work towards preserving and promoting the rich cultural heritage of India through various activities and initiatives. Here are some notable examples:

1. Textile and Handloom Development Organizations: Government bodies like the Ministry of Textiles in India and organizations such as the Handloom Export Promotion Council (HEPC) and Handloom Development Corporation (HDC) work towards the development and promotion of traditional Indian textiles and handloom products. They provide support to weavers and artisans, organize exhibitions and trade fairs, and facilitate marketing and export of traditional Indian attire.

2. Fashion Weeks and Festivals: Fashion weeks and festivals like Lakme Fashion Week, Amazon India Fashion Week, and India Fashion Week showcase traditional Indian attire and provide a platform for designers to exhibit their creations. These events help in promoting traditional Indian textiles, craftsmanship, and design techniques, while also fostering collaborations between designers, artisans, and the fashion industry.

3. Craft Revival Organizations: Organizations like Craft Council of India (CCI) and Dastkari Haat Samiti work towards reviving and promoting traditional crafts and

artisanal skills. They support artisans and craftspeople by providing training, marketing platforms, and creating awareness about the significance of traditional attire and handicrafts.

4. Non-Governmental Organizations (NGOs): Various NGOs are dedicated to promoting traditional Indian attire and empowering artisans. Organizations like SEWA (Self Employed Women's Association), Kala Raksha, and URMUL Trust work towards preserving traditional crafts, providing livelihood opportunities to artisans, and promoting ethical and sustainable practices in the textile industry.

5. Cultural and Educational Institutions: Cultural and educational institutions play a crucial role in promoting traditional attire through research, documentation, and education. Institutions like the National Institute of Fashion Technology (NIFT), National Institute of Design (NID), and Indian Council for Cultural Relations (ICCR) contribute to the preservation and promotion of traditional Indian attire through academic programs, exhibitions, and cultural exchange initiatives.

6. Online Platforms and E-commerce Websites: Several online platforms and e-commerce websites focus on promoting traditional Indian attire. These platforms provide a global reach for artisans and weavers, enabling them to showcase and sell their products to a wider audience. They also create awareness about the cultural significance of traditional attire and encourage its adoption.

These organizations and initiatives play a vital role in preserving, promoting, and sustaining traditional Indian attire. Their efforts contribute to the recognition and appreciation of the craftsmanship, cultural heritage, and beauty of traditional Indian clothing.

Government support and cultural festivals

Government support and cultural festivals are significant in promoting traditional Indian attire. The Indian government recognizes the cultural and economic importance of traditional attire and provides support through various initiatives. Here are some ways in which the government promotes traditional Indian clothing:

1. Financial Support: The government provides financial assistance, subsidies, and loans to weavers, artisans, and craftsmen involved in the production of traditional Indian attire. This support helps in sustaining their livelihoods and encourages the continuation of traditional crafts.

2. Design and Development Centers: The government has established design and development centers across the country to provide technical assistance and training to artisans and weavers. These centers focus on skill development, product innovation, and improving the quality of traditional attire.

3. Handloom Mark and Geographical Indications: The government has introduced the Handloom Mark and Geographical Indications (GI) for certain traditional fabrics and textiles. The Handloom Mark certifies the authenticity and quality of handloom products, while GI provides legal protection to specific regional textile products, ensuring their uniqueness and preventing unauthorized imitations.

4. National Handloom Day: The Indian government has designated August 7th as National Handloom Day to

promote handloom products and raise awareness about the significance of traditional Indian attire. Various events and campaigns are organized on this day to celebrate the rich heritage of handloom weaving.

5. Cultural Festivals: India is known for its vibrant cultural festivals that showcase traditional attire. Festivals like Navratri, Diwali, Pongal, Baisakhi, and Durga Puja provide platforms for people to adorn themselves in traditional clothing. These festivals highlight the diversity and richness of Indian culture and serve as a means of preserving and promoting traditional attire.

6. Government-Sponsored Exhibitions and Trade Fairs: The government organizes exhibitions and trade fairs at national and international levels to promote traditional Indian attire. These events bring together weavers, artisans, designers, and buyers, providing a platform for showcasing and marketing traditional clothing.

Government support and cultural festivals play a crucial role in preserving and promoting traditional Indian attire. They not only provide economic support but also create awareness and pride in the cultural heritage associated with traditional clothing. Through these efforts, the government contributes to the sustainability and continued relevance of traditional Indian attire.

Fashion shows and exhibitions showcasing traditional attire

Fashion shows and exhibitions showcasing traditional attire play a vital role in promoting and celebrating the rich cultural heritage of traditional Indian clothing. These events provide a platform for designers, artisans, and craftsmen to showcase their talent, creativity, and innovation in traditional fashion. Here are some key aspects of fashion shows and exhibitions focused on traditional attire:

1. Showcasing Traditional Designs: Fashion shows and exhibitions offer a platform for designers to present their collections inspired by traditional Indian attire. They blend traditional elements with contemporary aesthetics, creating a fusion that appeals to a wide range of audiences.

2. Reviving Traditional Techniques: These events often highlight the use of traditional weaving, embroidery, and dyeing techniques in creating unique and exquisite garments. By showcasing these techniques, fashion shows and exhibitions contribute to the revival and preservation of traditional craftsmanship.

3. Promoting Regional Diversity: India is a land of diverse cultures and traditions, each with its unique style of clothing. Fashion shows and exhibitions provide an opportunity to showcase the regional diversity of traditional attire, celebrating the distinct identities of different communities and regions.

4. Bridging Tradition and Modernity: Many fashion shows

and exhibitions explore the intersection of traditional and modern fashion. They present traditional attire in contemporary ways, catering to the evolving tastes and preferences of modern consumers. This helps in keeping traditional attire relevant and appealing to younger generations.

5. Encouraging Collaboration: Fashion shows and exhibitions often foster collaboration between designers, artisans, and craftsmen. This collaboration enables the exchange of ideas, skills, and techniques, leading to innovation in traditional fashion. It also creates opportunities for artisans to access new markets and gain recognition for their craftsmanship.

6. Promoting Sustainable Fashion: Traditional attire is often crafted using eco-friendly and sustainable practices. Fashion shows and exhibitions focused on traditional clothing emphasize the importance of sustainable fashion and promote the use of natural fibers, organic dyes, and ethical production processes.

Fashion shows and exhibitions showcasing traditional attire serve as a platform for cultural expression, creativity, and business opportunities. They play a crucial role in raising awareness about the beauty and significance of traditional Indian clothing, both within India and on the global stage. By bridging the gap between tradition and modernity, these events contribute to the preservation, promotion, and evolution of traditional attire.

Dressing for different occasions and events

Traditional Indian attire offers a wide range of options for dressing up for various occasions and events. Here are some guidelines on how to dress for different occasions:

1. Festivals and Religious Ceremonies: Festivals like Diwali, Holi, Eid, and Navratri, as well as religious ceremonies, call for traditional attire. Men can opt for a kurta-pajama or sherwani with intricate embroidery and embellishments. Pair it with a matching or contrasting stole and traditional footwear like mojris or juttis.

2. Weddings and Celebrations: Indian weddings are known for their grandeur and vibrant celebrations. Men can choose to wear a traditional sherwani, achkan, or bandhgala suit with heavy embroidery or embellishments. Pair it with a churidar or dhoti, and complete the look with a turban or an embellished pagdi. Accessorize with a brooch, traditional necklace, and ethnic footwear.

3. Formal and Business Events: For formal and business events, men can opt for a tailored bandhgala suit or a well-fitted Western suit with a touch of Indian aesthetics. Pair it with formal trousers or churidar and dress shoes. Add a pocket square or a lapel pin to add a dash of style to the outfit.

4. Casual Outings and Gatherings: For casual outings and gatherings, men can go for a simple yet elegant look. A well-fitted kurta or a casual shirt paired with jeans or trousers can be a comfortable and stylish choice. Add a Nehru jacket or a waistcoat to elevate the look.

5. Cultural Performances and Art Events: Attending cultural performances or art events provide an opportunity to showcase traditional attire with a creative twist. Men can experiment with fusion outfits by pairing a traditional kurta or shirt with dhoti-style pants, asymmetrical jackets, or draped scarves.

6. Traditional Day at Work or College: On occasions like traditional day at work or college, men can wear a kurta or a kurta-pajama combination. Opt for vibrant colors, unique prints, or subtle embroidery to showcase your style while maintaining the traditional essence.

Remember to choose the appropriate fabric, colors, and embellishments based on the occasion and the level of formality. Accessorize your outfits with traditional jewelry, pocket squares, turbans, or stoles to complete the look. Overall, dressing for different occasions in traditional Indian attire allows you to embrace the cultural heritage while expressing your personal style.

Matching accessories and footwear

When it comes to traditional Indian attire for men, matching accessories and footwear play an important role in completing the overall look. Here are some suggestions for matching accessories and footwear:

1. Turban or Pagdi: If you are wearing traditional headgear like a turban or pagdi, make sure it complements the color and style of your outfit. You can choose a matching or contrasting color, and consider adding embellishments or brooches to enhance the look.

2. Stole or Dupatta: A stole or dupatta is a versatile accessory that can add elegance to your attire. Choose a stole or dupatta that matches or complements the colors and patterns of your outfit. You can drape it around your shoulders or use it as a stylish accessory by draping it over one shoulder or around your neck.

3. Jewelry: Traditional Indian jewelry can enhance the overall look of your attire. You can opt for a necklace, pendant, or chain that complements your outfit. Pay attention to the metal and design of the jewelry to ensure it matches the style of your attire.

4. Footwear: Traditional Indian footwear options like mojris, juttis, kolhapuris, or sandals are popular choices for completing the traditional look. Choose footwear that matches the color and style of your outfit. Opt for comfortable yet stylish footwear that complements the occasion and your personal style.

5. Waistcoat or Nehru Jacket: If you are wearing a waistcoat or Nehru jacket, make sure it matches the

color and fabric of your outfit. You can choose a contrasting color to add a pop of style, or opt for a matching color for a more coordinated look.

6. Pocket Square or Lapel Pin: Adding a pocket square or lapel pin to your outfit can elevate the overall look. Choose a pocket square or lapel pin that complements the colors and patterns of your attire. Experiment with different folds and styles for the pocket square to add a touch of sophistication.

Remember, the key is to match the accessories and footwear with the colors, patterns, and overall style of your traditional attire. Pay attention to the occasion and your personal style preferences while selecting the accessories and footwear to create a cohesive and stylish look.

Tips for maintaining and caring for traditional attire

Maintaining and caring for traditional attire is crucial to preserve its beauty and longevity. Here are some tips to help you keep your traditional Indian attire in excellent condition:

1. Read and Follow Care Instructions: Different fabrics and embellishments require specific care. Read the care instructions provided with your attire and follow them diligently. Pay attention to recommended washing methods, ironing temperatures, and any other special instructions.

2. Hand Washing and Gentle Detergents: Hand washing is often the safest method for cleaning delicate traditional attire. Use a mild and gentle detergent suitable for the fabric. Avoid harsh chemicals, bleach, or strong detergents that can damage the fabric or color.

3. Color Separation: When washing your traditional attire, separate light and dark colors to prevent color bleeding. This is especially important for attires with vibrant or rich colors. Consider using color-catching sheets or color-protecting detergents to minimize color transfer.

4. Gentle Handling: Treat your traditional attire with care to avoid stretching, tearing, or damaging delicate embellishments. Gently hand wash or gently machine wash using the delicate cycle. Avoid wringing or twisting the fabric, as it can lead to deformation.

5. Drying Techniques: Air drying is generally the safest method for drying traditional attire. Hang the garments

on a padded hanger or lay them flat on a clean surface to prevent stretching. Avoid direct sunlight, as it can fade the colors. For delicate fabrics, consider placing a clean cloth over the attire while ironing to protect it.

6. Ironing: Use a low to medium heat setting while ironing your traditional attire. Test a small, inconspicuous area before ironing the entire garment. Use a pressing cloth or iron the attire inside out to prevent direct contact between the iron and the fabric.

7. Storage: Proper storage is crucial for maintaining the shape and condition of your traditional attire. Clean and completely dry the garments before storing them. Use acid-free tissue paper or clean cotton fabric to wrap delicate embellishments. Store in a cool, dry place away from direct sunlight and extreme temperatures. Avoid hanging heavy garments to prevent stretching.

8. Professional Cleaning: For heavily embellished or intricate traditional attire, consider professional cleaning services. They have experience in handling delicate fabrics and intricate designs, ensuring proper care and maintenance.

9. Regular Inspections: Regularly inspect your traditional attire for any signs of damage, loose threads, or missing embellishments. Promptly address any issues to prevent further damage and maintain the overall integrity of the garment.

By following these tips, you can ensure that your traditional Indian attire remains in excellent condition for years to come. Remember, proper care and maintenance not only preserve the beauty of your attire but also honor the cultural significance it holds.

Reflection on the significance of traditional Indian attire for men

Traditional Indian attire for men holds immense significance as it represents the rich cultural heritage and diversity of India. It serves as a powerful symbol of identity, reflecting regional customs, religious beliefs, and social status. The attire not only embodies centuries-old craftsmanship and artistry but also carries stories of ancestral traditions and historical events.

Wearing traditional Indian attire allows men to connect with their roots, showcasing their pride in their heritage. It serves as a means of expressing cultural belonging and a way to preserve and promote Indian traditions. The intricate designs, vibrant colors, and unique patterns of traditional garments captivate the imagination and add a touch of elegance and sophistication to any occasion.

Furthermore, traditional Indian attire encourages sustainability and ethical fashion practices. Many of these garments are handmade, using age-old techniques that have been passed down through generations. By embracing traditional attire, men support local artisans and weavers, contributing to the preservation of traditional crafts and providing livelihood opportunities in rural communities.

Traditional Indian attire also transcends borders, attracting global attention and admiration. Bollywood films and international fashion runways have showcased the beauty and versatility of Indian garments, amplifying their popularity and influencing fashion trends worldwide. This cross-cultural exchange not only creates opportunities for Indian designers and artisans but also fosters a deeper appreciation for the artistry and craftsmanship of traditional Indian attire.

In conclusion, traditional Indian attire for men is more than just clothing; it is a tangible representation of India's rich cultural heritage and a source of immense pride. Its significance lies in preserving traditions, supporting local artisans, promoting sustainable fashion practices, and fostering a sense of identity and connection to one's roots. As the world continues to embrace diversity and cultural appreciation, traditional Indian attire remains an enduring symbol of elegance, tradition, and timeless style.

Call to embrace and preserve the rich heritage of Indian clothing

In a rapidly changing world, it is crucial to embrace and preserve the rich heritage of Indian clothing. Traditional attire holds the key to our cultural identity and serves as a tangible link to our ancestors and their customs. By wearing and promoting traditional Indian garments, we contribute to the preservation of centuries-old craftsmanship and keep our heritage alive.

Let us celebrate the diversity and uniqueness of Indian clothing, recognizing its significance beyond mere fashion trends. By embracing traditional attire, we honor the skill and artistry of our artisans and weavers who have dedicated their lives to perfecting these timeless creations. We support local economies and communities, ensuring the sustainability of traditional crafts.

Furthermore, by choosing traditional Indian attire, we stand against the homogenization of global fashion and promote cultural diversity. We show the world the beauty and elegance of our traditional garments, inviting others to appreciate and respect our rich heritage. In doing so, we create a platform for cross-cultural exchange and foster mutual understanding and appreciation.

Preserving our traditional clothing is an act of love and pride for our culture. It is a way to pass on our traditions to future generations and ensure that they continue to thrive. Let us cherish the stories woven into every thread, the vibrant colors that speak of our diversity, and the intricate patterns that reflect our customs and beliefs.

In this call to embrace and preserve our rich heritage of Indian clothing, let us wear our traditional attire with confidence, grace, and pride. Let us educate others about the significance and beauty of our garments. Let us support the artisans and designers who dedicate their lives to this craft. Together, we can ensure that the splendor of traditional Indian attire continues to shine bright for generations to come.

www.ingramcontent.com/pod-product-compliance
Lightning Source LLC
Chambersburg PA
CBHW070500220526
45466CB00004B/1906